Steam Memories: 1950's – 1960's

No. 45: East Coast Main L

David Dunn

ISBN 978-1-909625-04-4

INTRODUCTION

Leaving Selby behind, we cross the Ouse and head north to Chaloners Whin where the lines from Leeds and Sheffield join our route, although the layout suggests otherwise. There we can observe (through the magic of film) the modernisation of that important junction between the years 1949 and 1961. Onwards then to York, we get a chance to see various departing Up expresses starting to stretch their legs as they head through Holgate. Next we come to that most elegant and interesting of junctions York – described as the greatest intermediate junction and railway centre on the ECML – the former headquarters of the North Eastern Railway. Here we will take a look at not only the station but the engine sheds, and various items of rolling stock, besides other items of interest.

From York to Northallerton we will pass over what was historically one of the fastest sections of the ECML where the Pacifics could be safely opened up and usually make up some time which may have been lost elsewhere on the route.

Our arrival at Northallerton will be met by not only a clutch of railway enthusiasts but by a gathering of British Railways employees, who appear at first sight to outnumber the civilians on the platform. Now you wouldn't get that today!

Volume 5 will illustrate the route of the line to Newcastle, passing through Darlington and numerous other junctions of course. However, that is some distance away and there is much to see during this leg from Selby to Northallerton.

Thanks must go to the Armstrong Railway Photographic Trust (ARPT) for the use of their material. Thanks also to Graham Jelly for that last minute check when a few omissions were intercepted!

David Dunn, Cramlington, October 2013.

Cover Whilst a party of semi-interested onlookers observe the movements, Hull Botanic Gardens D49 No.62723 NOTTINGHAMSHIRE performs a spot of shunting at the north end of York station in the early 1950s. *C.J.B.Sanderson (ARPT)*.

Title Page Less than a year before its withdrawal, Thompson A2/2 No.60501 COCK O' THE NORTH prepares for a northbound departure from York on Wednesday 15th April 1959. York based, it was not the first among its sisters to face the axe. *I.W.Coulson (ARPT)*.

Printed and bound by The Amadeus Press, Cleckheaton, West Yorkshire

First published in the United Kingdom by Book Law Publications, 382 Carlton Hill, Nottingham, NG4 1JA

Stranger in town! Two actually! Darnall J11 No.64419 heads an RCTS railtour outing on 20th June 1954 – *South Yorkshire No.3* – and is seen at Selby awaiting relief by Darlington based J21 No.65078. The special was apparently running forty minutes late on arrival at Selby, the J11 was not in the best of health (it was due a major overhaul later in the year) and its itinerary after a late start from Sheffield waiting for a connection, was not an easy one and took in many goods lines as far east as Frodingham. The J21's job was to haul the train over the Derwent Valley Railway to York where the J11 would be waiting to work back to Sheffield. However, when the train ran into York from the Scarborough line – gained via Layerthorpe and the Foss Islands branch – it was over fifty minutes behind schedule because the DVLR itself was hardly the place to make up lost time but was ideal for losing more. At York V2 No.60847 ST. PETERS SCHOOL, YORK was awaiting the RCTS special with the same driver and fireman who had struggled with the J11. However, there was no holding back the pair with a decent locomotive and time was made up for much of the journey until signals started to mess things about from Mexborough onwards. Late arrival in Midland station at Sheffield did not seem to bother anyone and apparently a good day out was enjoyed by all. The only mystery to this compiler was how did the J21 get to Selby? Pure speculation perhaps but why not after hauling a new, Darlington-built 350 h.p. 0-6-0DE shunting locomotive some way towards its new home at New England? Note the twelve-wheel dining car in the middle of the formation. *J.W.Armstrong (ARPT)*.

This is Selby in the late summer of 1952 with a Down morning 'stopper' from Leeds about to get underway behind Neville Hill B16/1 No.61440. Again, we have no exact date but the 4-6-0 was in works at Darlington during June and July of that year for a Heavy Intermediate overhaul when paint would most certainly be applied to the engine and which explains the fairly clean condition in this illustration. (*left*) North Eastern water column at Selby station, 12th July 1964. Note the blistering paint climbing up the upper half of the column; at first glance it appears to be some carefully arranged far eastern script. That on the arm is pure English giving the makers name Garrick & Wardale? *both C.J.B.Sanderson (ARPT)*.

A quick look at Selby motive power depot would not go amiss during our short stay in the town. Located on the west side of the Leeds line, adjacent to the junction of the line from Doncaster, the shed consisted two 'square' roundhouses of standard North Eastern design. The first of the pair was opened in 1871 whilst this building was commissioned in 1898. On this, the fifth day of August 1956, the stalls in No.1 shed housed a typical assortment of engines found at the depot at that time, with an emphasis on the ancient. This little group were all Selby residents with Q6 No.63382 just getting into the frame on the left as two D20s hog the picture. No.62387 was by now coupled to one of the rebuilt tenders which had the same body style as the LNER Group Standard 3500 gallon tenders whilst retaining the original chassis. However, these rebuilt vehicles had 3900 gallon capacity. No.62378 remained with its NER tender but not for much longer because later in the year, on the day after Bonfire Night, the 4-4-0 was condemned just a few days short of its 50th year. No.62387 transferred to Alnmouth during the following June but it too was condemned three months later. It is interesting to note that Selby had been home to more than half of the sixty strong class – thirty-five engines – at one time or another, some more than once. Note the guard rails of the 50ft turntable which would more than likely have a modern day H&S official beaming, although some minor detail would probably have the appliance 'shut down' for modification! *C.J.B.Sanderson (ARPT).*

One of Selby's T1s, No.69921, runs up the shed yard away from No.2 shed (the oldest with a 42ft. turntable) on a rather damp 4th April 1959. This particular 4-8-0 was to be the last of its class, though not a Selby engine. Transferring to Tyne Dock on 13th September 1959, No.69921 remained operational until withdrawal in June 1961. Not the small size BR wheel and lion emblem which it kept to withdrawal. Of the fifteen members in the class, eight of them worked from Selby at different periods with the main employment at Gascoigne Wood yard. Standing in the background, Ivatt Cl.4 No.43123 was one of six of the 2-6-0s still allocated to 50C at this time although they would all move on when the shed closed on 13th September next. Altogether, ten of the useful Ivatt Cl.4s had been allocated at Selby since December 1950 when No.43096 arrived new; it was quickly followed by sisters 43097–43099 in the New Year. Others came and went but the depot managed to keep hold of that core half-a-dozen to closure. *C.J.B.Sanderson (ARPT)*.

Back to the station, we are just in time to view a bit of history in the making! On the occasion of the marriage of the Duke of York, at his namesake Minster during the summer of 1961, a number of special trains were run from London to York bringing dignitaries and guests, including H.M. the Queen, to the city. The trains each had A4 haulage and King's Cross shed certainly went to town cleaning their charges for the task which took place on that Thursday, the 8th June. No.60028 WALTER K.WHIGHAM headed the train with the Queen aboard and is seen passing through Selby on the Down main during the morning of the wedding day. Other A4s involved for the occasion were Nos.60003, 60014 (spare engine for the Royal Train), and 60015. No.60028 also had the distinction of working the first 1961 season Down ELIZABETHAN express on the following Monday 12th June; for the record No.60031 worked the first Up train. N.W.Skinner (ARPT).

A not so clean A4 No.60020 GUILLEMOT (a Gateshead engine) runs over the swing bridge spanning the Ouse at Selby with a Down express in the 1950s. The control cabin atop the opening span was typical NER design, similar to the one at Naburn to the north, and Sculcoates in Hull for instance. *J.W.Armstrong (ARPT)*.

The signals are informing us that an Up train is due for the Normanton route whilst a Down train is approaching from that same route. Luckily for the photographer, and us, another train from Leeds is traversing the Down Leeds line. The date is 29th July 1949 – a Friday – and we are at Chaloners Whin where the ECML joins two other important routes. From left to right the lines were arranged as follows: Up Doncaster and Selby diverging off to the left; Down Doncaster and Selby joining from the left (the 'senior' route here is the Normanton–York which was much older than the 1871–opened Barlby–Chaloners Whin section of the ECML); Up Normanton; Down Normanton with Stanier Class 5 No.44781 heading a passenger train; Up Leeds; and the Down Leeds line with B16 No.61440 heading a rag–bag assortment of ancient rolling stock, complete with a clerestory roofed brake. Note the mixture of upper and lower quadrant signals. What a fabulous location, at least in 1949. *K.H.Cockerill (ARPT)*.

9

On the same day a southbound passenger working was captured on film from the lineside near to the Fogmans' hut – note the all-important levers for placing the detonators onto the relevant rails, and the telephone connection on the upper left corner of the hut – where a lone fog signalman would sit a vigil for hours on end, employed on one of what was probably quite eerie, lonely but necessary tasks on the railways of the period. The train in view has a nice combination of motive power with another Class '5', Wakefield's No.45221 double-heading a Starbeck D20 No.E2369 with what appears to be a formation of non-corridor stock; a throwback to the days when everybody, it seems, had a strong constitution or at least required one! *K.H.Cockerill (ARPT)*.

Some twelve years later, and standing in the 'six-foot' between the Up and Down Doncaster (ECML) lines at Chaloners Whin, the photographer captures a southbound freight, consisting steel empties, negotiating the points between the Up Leeds line and the Up Normanton line behind Canklow based WD No.90719 on Tuesday 23rd May 1961. The road bridge in the background had by now been rebuilt from the girder parapet type bridge shown in the previous illustration to one consisting precast concrete beams (cast on site on the open ground to the right) with brick parapets. Note the difference in the smoke stains revealing that Up trains were working harder than Down trains. The bridge was still a splendid vantage point for photographers and enthusiasts observing this important junction. York was just two miles dead ahead from this location. In the distance colour light signalling can be seen and in the cess on the Up side can be seen newly laid cable troughs awaiting the cabling which would complete the upgrade of the signalling in this area. R.H.Leslie (ARPT).

11

No chance of standing in the same position for this one! Bristol Barrow Road 'Patriot' No.45504 ROYAL SIGNALS takes the Up Normanton line on the same day with a York–Bristol express. The exhaust is another sign of the adverse gradient at this location. During the twelve years from 1949 major changes had taken place to the signalling in the York area (the job had started north of York in 1933) and in particular to this section of railway around Chaloners Whin. In 1936 it was announced that a new signal box would be built in York which would control over thirty-three track miles and enable seven manual signal boxes to be closed, amongst them Chaloners Whin. Three and four aspect colour light signals would be used throughout with route indicators at certain locations. However, though the scheme was announced in 1936, it was slow to implement and with the coming of WW2 it was necessary to put it on hold until the end of hostilities. In the end, BR had to take on the project to its completion. So, one of the reasons that colour light signals can be seen in a number of these illustrations between Chaloners Whin and York, not to mention the renewal of the road bridge at the former location, is because of the long-winded implementation of the scheme. Nevertheless, although it speeded up the trains, and made life easier for BR, it did change

12 the skyline somewhat when all those semaphore signal gantries and manual boxes were taken down. Such is progress. *R.H.Leslie (ARPT)*.

Backtracking slightly onto the ECML immediately south of Chaloners Whin junction we meet a March based K3 No.61921 blasting around the bend and away from the junction with a southbound fitted freight from York Dringhouses to Whitemoor yard on 23rd May 1961. Readily apparent now are the wide open spaces where the semaphore signal gantry and the erstwhile signal box, surplus to the renewal and long-term modernisation of the signalling system in the area, once stood. Soon it would be the turn of the motive power to undergo massive change. What! It had already started!? *R.H.Leslie (ARPT)*.

Returning to semaphore days! Two northbound expresses run through the junction with totally different motive power. Coming off the ECML Peppercorn A1 No.60147, which has yet to be named, looks to be in typical Gateshead condition carrying a thick coating of grime. Representing the old LMS interests, a reasonably turned-out Bank Hall 'Jubilee' No.45698 MARS changes route from the Down Normanton onto the Down Leeds to allow the Down ECML express complete occupation of the Down main. It must have been quite disconcerting for both crews when approaching such a junction hoping that the signalmen had got it right! The signal in the background controlling both Down lines from the Normanton direction can be seen indicating the route taken by the 4-6-0. The date for this image is not logged but a few pointers might help with an approximate date: (1) The A1 was new in April 1949 and named NORTH EASTERN in March 1952 but it had spent all of that period at 52A. (2) Contractors appear to have set-up the site for casting the new bridge spans and storing all the necessary equipment required for the job. Completion of said bridge would be useful to know. *K.H.Cockerill (ARPT)*.

14

Pegged for the Doncaster route and with about fourteen on, York's Peppercorn A2 No.60534 IRISH ELEGANCE is working hard to get this formation moving at express speed as it approaches the aforementioned overbridge at Chaloners Whin on 29th July 1949. Again, another signal gantry reveals the Up direction routes prior to the junction proper. Note the colour light gantry erected approximately halfway between the two semaphore gantries. The proximity of the lineside residence here leaves one wondering about the noise and vibration experienced within that household virtually 364 days, and nights each year' K.H.Cockerill (ARPT).

It is now early September and the late afternoon sun gives this illustration a different perspective to that of the previous one. Thompson B1 No.61258 is on the Up Leeds line and has charge of a lightweight express on Saturday 9th September 1950. The train is another rather mixed combination with a former Great Central vehicle leading. The infant British Railways had much to do standardising the carriage fleet but it would be fifteen years or more before the majority of the pre-Grouping passenger stock was finally eliminated; we enjoyed the variety but the travelling public and BR operating staff were probably glad to see the back of them. The Neville Hill B1 was recently out from a General overhaul at Darlington (the workshops had responsibility for their own regional locomotive stock at the time, so that when No.61258 transferred to Doncaster shed in January 1952, its maintenance was then undertaken at Doncaster works). A minor point worth repeating is the fact that this particular 4-6-0 was the last of its class to be cut up at Doncaster. Note that the aforementioned bungalow is certainly well catered for regarding fireplaces; look at those fabulous chimney pots which would help the domestic fires draw your slippers off, if you weren't careful. K.H.Cockerill (ARPT).

16

Hughes-Fowler 'Crab' No.42756, with about ten bogies behind the tender, runs south through the junction on 9th September 1950. The train was a return excursion from Scarborough to Burton-on-Trent, which the 2-6-0 would have worked throughout. *K.H.Cockerill (ARPT)*.

How about this at the end of the garden? Relegated now to workings such of these, the GE Lines 'Brits' took a bit of a tumble from grace when the diesels arrived in East Anglia. The Norwich and Stratford engines which handled the Ipswich, Harwich and Norwich expresses out of Liverpool Street were all transferred to March, a depot more associated with freight than passenger work. On 23rd May 1961 No.70037 HEREWARD THE WAKE is in charge of a York–Whitemoor fitted freight, an almost daily occurrence with 31B having such a glut of the class resident. *R.H.Leslie (ARPT)*.

18

Steaming well, King's Cross A4 No.60003 ANDREW K.McKOSH departs from York and is passing the Holgate platforms with an 11–coach express for London on Saturday 18th August 1962. This same train was later photographed south of Grantham and the A4 still had lots of steam to spare. However, it was an early candidate for withdrawal and was condemned in the December. *N.W.Skinner (ARPT)*.

York was well blessed with yards during BR days – goods yards, carriage yards, engine yards, engineers yards – and each one held their own attractions to the fraternity known as railway enthusiasts. In August 1961 the Engineers yard at Holgate had amongst its delectations this little bundle of joy which was used to shunt the premises, therefore releasing a Capital stock locomotive for revenue earning work elsewhere. Departmental No.52 (formerly 11104) was a rather sophisticated machine in a simple sort of way, its buffering arrangement enabled it to handle standard wagons and the odd awkward vehicle which might be bufferless. Introduced in 1950 and weighing in at 11 tons, the four-wheel appliance was built by that well-known firm of Hibberd & Co. In appearance, it was a bit like a tractor on metal flanged wheels, chain driven by an internal combustion engine of English National design producing 52 brake horsepower at 1250 r.p.m. In essence, a simple version of a Sentinel! Note the elaborate lining around the cab; BR York seems to have been more aware then most places of its public image. The stabling shed in the right background was for those cold, damp nights and weekends when the little 0-4-0 was left on its own. *N.W.Skinner (ARPT)*.

All ten vehicles of the Down portion of *THE ELIZABETHAN* are visible in the illustration at Holgate on 7th August 1961. The premier A4 No.60014 SILVER LINK has total control of the train and is reducing speed ready for the run through the station. This Pacific was virtually working every other train on this service during August 1961. Note the crowd of admirers and enthusiasts on the Up platform. *N.W.Skinner (ARPT)*.

Coming thick and fast now as we approach York, the Up expresses are striding out after their stops or slow run-throughs of the station. This is one express which did run through York, and everywhere else too for that matter, *THE ELIZABETHAN* which on Monday 7th August 1961 had old favourite A4 No.60024 KINGFISHER in charge. *N.W.Skinner (ARPT)*.

The view from the Down platform at Holgate during the late afternoon of Saturday 21st May 1955 as Heaton based A3 No.60069 SCEPTRE departs for the south with a seemingly lightweight express. *C.J.B.Sanderson (ARPT)*.

The unmistakable vista of Holgate bridge announces our arrival in York on 25th August 1962 as A4 No.60015 QUICKSILVER strides out for the south after its station stop with a rather heavier express. The ornamental flower bed on the Up side embankment was a nice gesture to the travelling public during the days when horticultural excellence abounded all over the railway system; competitions were held annually to award prizes or certificates for the best station gardens or the best kept station (these usually also included a patch of earth with some nicely arranged flowers or shrubs). It would be a brave man who could say which region, in BR days, had the most 'well-kept station gardens' or indeed which had the best of them. The former LNER area stations did seem to excel in this line of 'green fingered(ness)' – see *Border Counties Railway Part 1** for instance – but then, on the other hand, there were some rather sorry looking stations which would have walked away with awards for the grottiest station of the year! *N.W.Skinner (ARPT).*

* Book Law Publications, 2013.

The south end of the York layout during the early spring of 1963, with BR Standard Cl.3 No.77013 heading south with an Engineers saloon! Curving off to the left of the picture are the goods avoiding lines which rejoined the main line at Skelton junction, just over a mile north of York station. In the centre background, and slightly to the left, are the various roundhouses and engine sheds which were of York & North Midland, or North Eastern lineage. Although in the main they appeared derelict and some even roofless, they were still in use up to this period as an overflow for the main depot at York North. Finally, the main line on which the Standard is running leads us to the passenger station with its sweeping arched roofs over curved platforms, an architectural delight if ever there was one and which thankfully survives today. The 2-6-0 is wearing a Scarborough 50E shedplate and although that depot was to close in April of that year, it was not unusual to find this engine at York on a regular basis whereby it would have worked in on a parcels or mail train from the seaside. The fact that the Cl.3 has been seconded to haul the saloon is also not surprising because York tended to use any decent engine it could lay its hands on for such duties including new ones en route from Doncaster or Darlington. *A.R.Thompson (ARPT)*.

25

The vast amount of freight which passed through York during the era of the steam locomotive must not be forgotten in this age when goods trains are seemingly less plentiful on most parts of the network. On 2nd September 1962 a typical Up goods working is captured on film joining the main line at Holgate bridge with WD 2-8-0 No.90518 (one of York's own this one) in charge. *N.W.Skinner (ARPT)*.

Running up the goods lines for a few hundred yards from whence the WD came, we get a closer view of the South shed roundhouses from a vantage point on the west side of the avoiding lines. The multi-pitched roofless building was opened in 1864 by the NER and when that company moved its locomotive facilities to York North in 1878, the roundhouse was leased to the Midland Railway. Roofless for a few years prior to its closure in 1961, it was demolished in 1963. To the right is another roundhouse, complete with conical roof, which was even older than the NER shed. This was opened in 1852 by the Y&NMR and, as can be seen, survived into that final decade of steam on BR. Up until 1921 it had a virtual twin located on its eastern side but that 1850 built shed was destroyed by fire in 1921. In the 1950s and 60s' there were nearly as many goods trains passing through here as passenger trains and the procession brought locomotives from far and wide including, latterly, in the early period of the 60s', Type 3 diesel locomotives (later to become Class 33) from the Southern Region which worked bulk cement trains right through from Kent. On this day the more usual make-up of goods vehicles, some displaying their contents, can be seen with a train of livestock wagons offering some real historical context. Sadly, none of the buildings, wagons, locomotives or much else in the fore and middle ground of this illustration survives today except perhaps some of the wagon-borne relay boxes. *J.W.Armstrong (ARPT)*.

Inside the roofless and largely unoccupied 1864 shed with empty and weed strewn stalls gathered around the 45ft. turntable. On an unknown date but circa 1961, J94 No.68046 stands on the exit road as if it was about to make the grand final departure from the empty shell. *R.F.Payne (ARPT)*.

28

Some years beforehand, on Saturday 29th July 1950, the shed just illustrated still had its rather ornamental roof largely intact, the larger holes were in fact ventilation aids. The two roundhouses form the backdrop for this forlorn looking Garratt – No.47980 – which was waiting to work home to Hasland after the weekend. This shed yard was the ideal location to stable these monster engines and although they were known to have stabled occasionally on the North shed, they only usually went there for coaling and servicing. The 2-6-0+0-6-2 is actually stabled on the tracks serving what was once the three-road Great Northern engine shed at York and which had been occupied by the LMS since 1932 – it would seem that these engines' great bulk and awkward dimensions had something to do with the LNER moving out in order to keep the Garratts out of the way of everywhere else! *K.H.Cockerill (ARPT)*.

Further up the yard on that dull and overcast Saturday in July 1950 was a Stanier 8F from Westhouses which had no doubt worked in with a mineral train. Once again filth rules the day although the front numberplate and shed plate are well depicted. The shed had been re-roofed by the LMS, the original hipped roof being in such a bad condition that it had to be demolished. The resultant new covering – which was somewhat unique to the railway world and more akin to the agricultural industry – is plain to see in this view. The broken glass in the multi-pane windows possibly stems from the air raids suffered by York during WW2 – the Baedeker raid of 29th April 1942 in particular – and which, in 1950 at least, had not been replaced. The hotchpotch of engine sheds are York South must have been extremely inconvenient in their layout from the day they were built up to the day they were demolished. *K.H.Cockerill (ARPT).*

The other end of the barn-like shed with a brick screen rather than timber forming the gable. The date is 13th April 1962 and BR Standard Cl.3 2-6-2T No.82028 from Malton is looking about as atrocious a steam locomotive could get, even then. This compiler is unsure whether the engine is stabled or stored at this time because even Malton depot was finding difficulty in fully employing these useful tanks. The presence of the 2-6-2T at York was a precursor of things to come and in April 1963 three members of the class, Nos.82027, 82028, and 82029, were allocated to York when Malton closed its doors for the last time. Whilst at 50A the trio did little of the work they were designed for and spent a lot of time in store or, reportedly, working Officer's specials; No.82028 may well have been overlooked for those duties. In September the York trio were transferred to the Southern Region and that was the end of their all too brief career on the NER. One of the ex-LMS Ivatt Cl.2 tank engines – in the same condition as our subject it appears – pokes out of the shed. This was a class which were quite elusive in this part of the world so may have been one of the few allocated to Malton at that time. *N.W.Skinner (ARPT)*.

Storage, mass storage! It happened at many engine sheds but none more so than York where there was in effect lots of space for storing the redundant steam locomotives. If this was a winter photograph such a situation could be regarded as normal because winter passenger services were not as numerous as the summertime peaks hence many locomotives were greased up and laid-up for the quiet months. However, the date of this illustration is 29th July. The clue is in the year – 1962! A bad time!? Yes, in the great scheme of things, because some of the mass 'culls' indeed the mass cull of the BR period took place in 1962. But luckily for Thompson B1 No.61240 HARRY HINCHLIFFE, all is not what it appears to be. The 4-6-0 was based at York during this period but it had also recently received a major overhaul at Darlington – 19th February to 28th March – so was good for another couple of years at least (such credentials however did not always ensure longevity in this decade). The chimney has been covered so somebody cared about the condition of the locomotive although three months accumulation of dirt has been allowed to gather. August, September, October, and most of November passed with the B1 still motionless here between the old roundhouses but on Sunday 25th November a transfer to Ardsley was signed and another four years of work was virtually guaranteed for Harry'. The end came at Wakefield on 6th December 1966. Besides the ex-works B1, York South shed was also home to the following stored but ex-works engines at this time: Nos.60887, 60895, 60939, 60982; an other B1 was 61039; WD 2-8-0s were also laid-up – 90467, 90571, 90578, and 90663. Note the gas lamp on the shed wall burning brightly; now about that gas bill! *N.W.Skinner (ARPT)*.

32

Three months earlier, on Friday 13th April 1962, further batches of locomotives were stored on the South shed yard in view of the station. Besides WD No.90424 there was a couple of fairly clean Pacifics, York's Peppercorn A1 No.60146 PEREGRINE amongst them. Neither of the identified engines were under threat at the time; indeed, the A1 had another three years operational life in front of it whilst the older WD 2-8-0 was a bit less fortunate being condemned in December 1963. On the Monday following this photographic recording, the A1 entered Doncaster 'Plant' works to receive its last General overhaul, complete with a refurbished boiler. *N.W.Skinner (ARPT)*.

Queen Street was another of the array of engine sheds located at York. This one was on the Up side of the main line at the south end of the station and was ideal for positioning the main line pilot during its long waiting hours. On 19th May 1952 Thompson A2/3 No.60524 HERRINGBONE had the duty and was suitably prepared. This Pacific was one of Thompson's longer lasting engines by dint of the fact that it was transferred to Scotland in December 1962 and managed to serve three different depots, the last being Polmadie of all places. The shed here was typical for York in that its history was hardly straightforward. Converted from what had once been the boiler shop of the old works, the place was opened in 1909 and consisted four roads to house both Great Central and Great Eastern locomotives alongside Lancashire & Yorkshire engines (off the Liverpool–Newcastle passenger workings in particular). In 1923 the LNER Group engines moved across to the South shed roundhouse whilst the Midland engines using that place vacated and moved to Queen Street which then became the main LMS shed in the city. By nationalisation former LMS engines working into York used both North and South sheds and Queen Street was largely abandoned except for usage such as this. *C.J.B.Sanderson (ARPT)*.

34

Now here is an interesting view not often photographed. We are at the south side of the Queen Street engine shed on 19th May 1952 with D20 No.62378 which was standing on the turntable road – the 50ft diameter table was located immediately behind the tender, between the two buildings – and waiting for a working which would take the 4-4-0 home to Selby. The building in the background was the former wagon shop which had been converted into a gymnasium by 1935 but what its post-war purpose was is unknown. The engine is standing in the space formerly occupied by the fitting shop of the old works, evidence of the shed wall once being an internal structure is plain to see. The original York Museum was housed in the building behind the photographer. Enough of the locomotive facilities for now, its time to look at the station and the trains it served. *C.J.B.Sanderson (ARPT).*

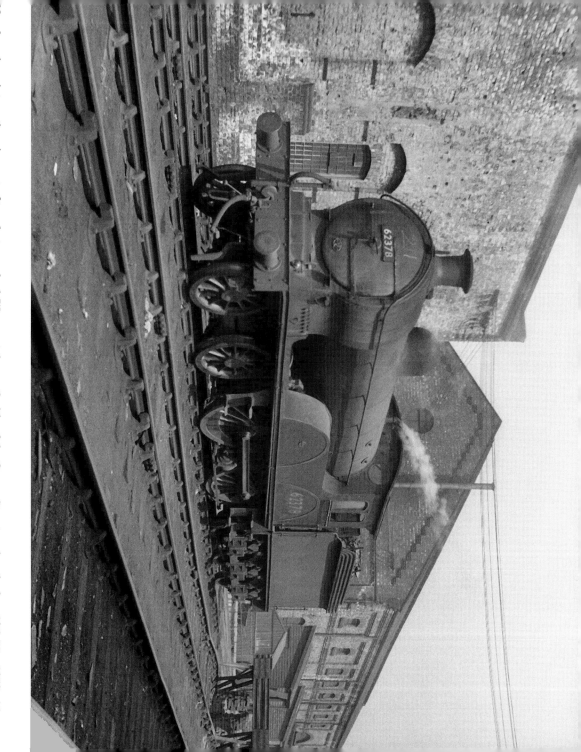

With 188 miles covered and signalled for a clear road, the heavily loaded Down *FLYING SCOTSMAN*, with record breaking A4 No.22 *MALLARD* in charge, begins its run through York station on Saturday 25th September 1948. Heading in a south-west north-east direction at this point, the train will have negotiated a near 90 degree change in direction by the time it exits the station. Slow progress here but No.22 will soon be on the forty-mile racetrack towards Darlington. *J.W.Armstrong (ARPT)*.

Now for a quick deviation from the main line! Just inside the city wall from the 'new' (1877) York station stood the 'old' Y&NMR station which had long been out of use for passenger traffic when BR came into being. However, it was a useful piece of real estate in a city such as York where land inside the city walls was/is rather expensive. The magnificent building dominating the background was the former North Eastern Railway headquarters which over the years has had a similar standing on an Area or Regional basis. However, in the early 1950s BR were enthusiastically staging exhibitions throughout the country to show off their latest motive power and rolling stock and from the Monday 4th to Saturday 16th June 1951, they exhibited some old and new stock at a gathering organised to celebrate York's contribution to the Festival of Britain. Locomotives on display were the first of British Railways Standard class locomotives No.70000 BRITANNIA itself; world record holder A4 No.60022 MALLARD; fairly new but hardly used yet, EM1 Bo-Bo electric No.26014; preserved GNR Atlantic No.251; and fresh from its plinth at Darlington station, LOCOMOTION. The rolling stock included various ancient Royal carriages plus some of the latest vehicles built by BR including a recently built First class Sleeper, and a Post Office – GPO – Sorting van. *J.W.Armstrong (ARPT)*.

37

Of the exhibits at the 1951 'bash', No.70000 reportedly worked its passage to York via King's Cross when, on Tuesday 29th May it hauled the 8.30 a.m. Likewise, it worked home on Monday 18th June hauling the 5.34 p.m. ex Newcastle express. Eastern Region (Great Eastern lines) 'Britannia's' were no strangers to York over the years and regular daily workings on express's from Colchester, for instance, brought them to the city. However, No.70007 COEUR-DE-LION's visit on Sunday 23rd October 1960 was in conjunction with a running-in turn from Doncaster after repair at the Plant works. Although not visible here, the Pacific had been fitted with a speedometer on its left rear flank but the classification of the overhaul which took it to Doncaster is not known. Note the somewhat empty tender. *N.W.Skinner (ARPT)*.

(above) Two D49s, Nos.62731 SELKIRKSHIRE (50A York) and 62742 THE BRAES OF DERWENT (50A) carry out a spot of shunting at the south end of the station in 1950. Both locomotives are in deplorable condition but they were due for works attention by the end of the year. The large brick building dominating the background is the former Queen Street locomotive erecting shops. *J.W.Hague.*

(below) A King's Cross–Newcastle express gets underway on Saturday 2nd September 1961 behind Darlington based V2 No.60809 THE SNAPPER, THE EAST YORKSHIRE REGIMENT, THE DUKE OF YORK'S OWN (not quite the longest name in the class, that was carried by No.60835, but it was certainly a mouth full). Some ten weeks after this scene was recorded, No.60809 entered the works at Darlington to undergo a two-month long Casual Heavy overhaul when separate cylinders were fitted. This V2 was actually one of the unlucky ones which ended up at Swindon for cutting up. *N.W.Skinner (ARPT).*

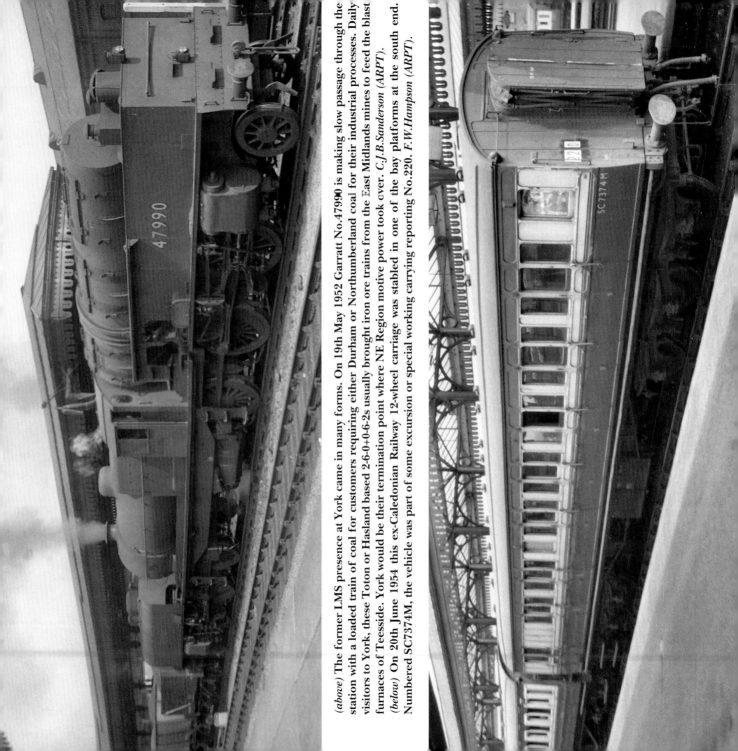

(*above*) The former LMS presence at York came in many forms. On 19th May 1952 Garratt No.47990 is making slow passage through the station with a loaded train of coal for customers requiring either Durham or Northumberland coal for their industrial processes. Daily visitors to York, these Toton or Hasland based 2-6-0+0-6-2s usually brought iron ore trains from the East Midlands mines to feed the blast furnaces of Teesside. York would be their termination point where NE Region motive power took over. *C.J.B.Sanderson (ARPT)*.

(*below*) On 20th June 1954 this ex-Caledonian Railway 12-wheel carriage was stabled in one of the bay platforms at the south end. Numbered SC7374M, the vehicle was part of some excursion or special working carrying reporting No.220. *F.W.Hampson (ARPT)*.

Wearing the grime usually associated with Gateshead steeds, Peppercorn A1 No.60155 BORDERER waits for the right-away at York with an afternoon Newcastle-King's Cross express on Monday 10th June 1957. *D.Fairley (ARPT)*.

Carrying on the LMS theme! Bank Hall 'Jubilees' and 'Patriots' were also daily visitors to York having worked in on the Liverpool (Exchange)–Newcastle (Central) expresses. At York North Eastern Region motive power took over the working whilst the 4-6-0s retired to North shed for servicing and to await a return working. 'Jubilee' No.45717 DAUNTLESS has done all of the procedures required before returning home and here it waits at York station during the afternoon of Sunday 9th August 1959 to take over the next Newcastle–Liverpool express. It appears that a couple of vans are already attached and will accompany the train to its destination on the west coast. This engine spent the whole of its life working from Lancashire sheds starting at Blackpool in July 1936, on to Southport in September 1939, Newton Heath from June 1940, back to Southport in April 1948 and finally Bank Hall six months later. Coupled to a low capacity Fowler type tender for much of its existence, DAUNTLESS had managed to acquire one of the intended Stanier tenders (No.10750) during a Heavy Intermediate overhaul just fourteen weeks before this scene was captured on film. *N.W.Skinner (ARPT)*.

A wheeltapper starts his long walk to the rear of this southbound working which has stopped at York on the afternoon of Sunday 20th July 1958. Although there was plenty of time to do so at this York stop (Sunday timings allowed plenty of time for station stops, and for the whole journey), the position of the engine reveals that the tender does not require topping up as the crew has obviously managed to fill the tank on the water troughs en route from Newcastle. A4 No.60016 SILVER KING (one of the original Hornby-Dublo A4s) is looking resplendent in the summer sunshine which is surprising really because it was a Gateshead engine at this time – since January 1945 in fact – and would remain so until October 1963 when it transferred to Scotland for an extra lease of life. Such was 52A's reputation for providing filthy engines for their express workings, I had to check the records to see if this A4 had recently been in shops for overhaul but it had not. On the contrary, within six weeks it was due to enter Doncaster shops for a General overhaul. So, assume nowt! Not to put a dampener on the *unusual* – though it had nothing to do with Gateshead – note the BR crest! *C.J.B.Sanderson (ARPT).*

(above) 29th July 1950. York station pilot J71 No.68286 looks resplendent in the green lined livery which it had acquired during a General overhaul at Gateshead at the end of 1949. Prior to this livery, the 0-6-0T had worn the LNER fully lined green which had been applied at Darlington in May 1947 (it had been at York for most of its life and been fitted with a vacuum ejector in 1909 for pilot work). No.68286 was the only J71 to be accorded green livery by either the LNER or BR. The Darlington version of the lining also included the splasher and the ends of the front bufferbeam, whereas Gateshead left those areas out of the scheme; still, it looked rather grand in a period when most locomotives were lucky if they were cleaned. Sadly, the J71 was condemned during a visit to Darlington in June 1952. *K.H.Cockerill (ARPT).*

(left) A little gem from 11th July 1964. One of the original North Eastern luggage barrows, No.3666 is posed for its photograph but look at the broken left handle – surely a death sentence in the era when everything old and steamy was being destroyed. *C.J.B. Sanderson (ARPT).*

Bringing a touch of US railroading to the United Kingdom, Derby based BR Standard Class 5 No.73030 stands at the head of a train from the London Midland Region which was bound for the east coast on Sunday 20th June 1954. Used by Derby, or rather the LMR CME, to conduct road tests in conjunction with the Westinghouse air brake equipment, which is largely noticeable at the front end, the 4-6-0 undertook normal duties between those tests and on this Sunday it has a Scarborough excursion in tow and is awaiting the signal on platform 14 to proceed over the crossing at the north end of York station to gain the road to the coast. Aesthetically, another set of air pumps on the left side of the smokebox would have balanced the locomotive better and given a more authentic US appearance; the large air storage tank beneath the running plate was actually mirrored on the left side of the engine. As things turned out, the Westinghouse pump was only a 'temporary' measure and had been fitted when the locomotive was new in June 1953, prior to it entering Rugby testing station that summer for steaming tests. Sister No.73031 was also fitted with Westinghouse equipment and subjected to similar testing at Rugby. Both engines took part in road tests either singly or coupled together on Toton-Brent fitted coal trains during 1954 and 1955. No.73031 had its pump and air tanks removed in March 1956. No.73030 lost its pump in November 1955 after the tests were long concluded. No.73031 had its pump and air tanks removed in March 1956. Note the grimy condition of the engine. Did public image not matter to BR or were they so arrogant as to think that such things didn't matter. *F.W.Hampson (ARPT)*.

Now that we are in former North Eastern territory D20 class will figure largely as we illustrate the journey northwards. Still at York, we show a rather decrepit looking (although, apparently steaming well) No.62395 standing at the head of a 'stopper' on 21st May 1955. The Selby 4-4-0 had last been to works for a major overhaul in June 1953 and would not venture into the shops again until condemned in November 1957. So, for the next two and a half years following this photographic recording, shed staff would have the job of keeping the D20 maintained and roadworthy. York got that responsibility from December 1956 and then in June 1957 it was transferred to Alnmouth, which had, it seems, become a magnet for the surviving members of the class. It is worth mentioning that the engines of this class had once worked the fastest, heaviest and most important expresses originating in or passing through NER territory; right up to Grouping they could be found working expresses on the ECML such was their usefulness. However, evolution takes its toll on the best and thirty-odd years after their greatest triumphs the D20 had settled into working secondary passenger services and parcels trains. No.62395, along with five remaining members of D20 class were all withdrawn in 1957, our subject was actually condemned on shed at Alnmouth on 20th November. In December the 4-4-0 was towed away to works for scrapping but before the final act the engine and tender were repainted in unlined black when received at Darlington, the splasher beadings were polished, and the new BR crest applied to the tender. However, the make-up was to the front and one side of the locomotive only, simply for official photographic purposes. Ironically, by design or by chance, the left side of the engine was chosen for the portrait and the crest on display was the correct version with the left facing lion. *C.J.B.Sanderson (ARPT)*.

A4 No.60008 DWIGHT D.EISENHOWER starts away from the York stop with the Down *TEES-TYNE PULLMAN* on an unknown date but circa mid-50s' (after June 1954 and before April 1957), next stop Darlington. It was only the Down working which stopped at York, the morning Up train ran non-stop from Darlington to King's Cross. Whatever the date, the condition of the engine gives the impression that it was not a Gateshead based locomotive, and you would be correct in thinking such. This Pullman train was a BR innovation and the first service ran in September 1948, loading to eight vehicles. In the left background stands the great bulk of the North Eastern's Royal Station Hotel which is still in business, and commanding a superb view of the station and its environs. *R.F.Payne (ARPT)*.

Striding out for the north! After a stop at York, A4 No.60032 GANNET resumes its journey on Monday 13th August 1962. The diamond crossing was created to enable trains to access the Scarborough line from the west side of the station. *I.S.Carr (ARPT)*.

48

Northbound departure, June 1959! With the evening sun beginning to cast long shadows and produce some exquisite – even in monochrome – light tones, a double-headed express gets underway and crosses over the Scarborough lines. The motive power consists of Tweedmouth based V2 No.60865 and New England's A2/3 No.60500 EDWARD THOMPSON, which was quite a combination from whatever angle you look at it. However, as if to reflect the mood of the moment, the locomotives appear to be making a somewhat gentile exit from the station. *A.R.Thompson (ARPT)*.

Another undated but nevertheless dramatic photograph showing Peppercorn A2 No.525 A.H.PEPPERCORN departing from York on a fine summer evening with a Down express circa 1948 whilst in the background the Minster views proceedings from afar. This locomotive was essentially the final one built by the LNER and was put into traffic on Christmas Eve 1947, the first of Peppercorn's Pacifics. Note that a shedplate has yet to be fitted – the Eastern and North Eastern regions were slow in getting the codes finalised in the first place, never mind casting thousands of plates with a myriad of codes – and renumbering of the Pacific was also yet to take place (August 1949) including having a front numberplate fitted (even more casting). *J.W.Armstrong (ARPT)*.

The words 'Gresley' and 'York' come to mind. This trio of V2s – 60847, 60828, and 60856 – were captured on film on 28th April 1963 on the North shed yard. They were in steam and all had outside steam pipes and had retained their top lamp irons in the original position; obviously there was little intention of sending any of this lot 'under the wires' before withdrawal. All three were York engines, two of them would last out until 1965 and end up in the hands of private scrapyards; the other would be condemned in 1964 and make the long journey to Swindon where the lasts rites were given. *A.R.Thompson (ARPT)*.

51

The great sweep of the 1957-59 rebuilding of the four roundhouse sheds which made up the York North (Leeman Road) depot still required tie-bars within the roof units such was their span. No.1 and No.2 sheds became a straight shed and were converted into a repair shop, later becoming a diesel depot. This view of 11th May 1967 is looking over a rather empty building with most of the former occupants either scrapped or about to get the axe. The depot itself was about to close to steam and these few remaining occupants sent away. One of the Independent snow ploughs built by the North Eastern Railway languishes on a stabling road as if anticipating the future use of this building, and its own preservation. Taking centre stage is BR Standard Cl.3 No.77012 whose sister we met at Holgate earlier; the 2-6-0 was still in Operating Stock but not for much longer because it was condemned in June (it had already been through that process in 1965 when it was withdrawn and then re-instated). There were, at this time in 1967, plans to preserve the Standard but they came to nothing and the BR Standard Cl.3 would be left unrepresented in the world of preserved steam locomotives. Of course, we all know what happened in 1975 at this venue, and the later drastic rebuilding required because of the concrete cancer riddling the roof beams. The place has certainly undergone some transformations since it was first opened in 1878. *Trevor Ermel (ARPT)*.

It is 20th June 1954 and we are in a section of the shed which has yet to be rebuilt, the original tie-bars of the 1878 roof looking like a spiders web of steel and cast-iron. This is No.3 shed, the one which was nearest to Leeman Road, where its stabling roads were accessible only through the later built No.4 shed (1915) and, for the smaller engines, through No.2 shed (also 1878). This shed would be re-roofed in 1959 in conjunction with the 1915 shed. Meanwhile, the shed pilot, Y8 No.8091, was making a meal of hanging on to its LNER number although it is just possible to see that the letters LNER had been painted over. On the day that this scene was recorded the little 0-4-0 was taken into Departmental Stock and renumbered in the Departmental series becoming No.55 during August. Because of its job – its diminutive size gave it access to any part of the shed complex – a vacuum ejector had been fitted in 1943, on transfer from Hull Dairycoates to York, to enable it to move vacuum fitted engines about the shed. One rather poignant fitting which it acquired on arrival at York was the chime whistle from A4 No.4469, the Pacific which had been destroyed in May 1942 during an air raid on the city; the whistle was removed by 1946 and it would be interesting to know what happened to that. Outlasting all four of its siblings, No.8091 was eventually withdrawn on 22nd November 1956, aged sixty-six years. *F.W.Hampson (ARPT)*.

53

Another view inside the rebuilt shed from 26th September 1964 with active locomotives, smoke and steam. Nothing glamorous about the locomotives ringing the turntable pit: one B1 No.61198, two K1s, No.62047 and an unidentified example, and an Ivatt Cl.4 'Flying Pig' No.43126. Oh to see such mediocrity today. *N.W.Skinner (ARPT)*.

Planned maintenance or fixing a broken component? No matter for what reason a mechanical coaling plant was out of action, it created chaos anyway at any shed. At an establishment as busy as York it was virtually catastrophic. The date when this scene was enacted was 23rd October 1960, a Sunday. It was the ideal day when jobs such as that shown could be hurriedly taken care of without too much disruption; assuming that it was a planned repair. If a breakdown had occurred it could be many days before the plant was operational again – perish the thought. However, the fitters who took care of such things were good at working under pressure, with the minimum of safeguards and in awkward and cramped conditions. The steam powered crane, which looks as dirty as most of the locomotives on shed, appears inadequate for the task but it was obviously ideal; anything outside of its lifting capacity would have brought the depot's Breakdown crane into play and that could be another headache for the operations people; note how the crane was secured to the running rails at both ends of the carriage, no outriggers here just good old clamps. The cables laid in the cess behind the crane have probably been taken off the tower temporarily, which suggests that the job was a bit more than a day long and may well have involved the whole weekend. *N.W.Skinner (ARPT)*.

55

Besides the locomotives visiting York from the LM Region, they had as many from the Eastern Region and here during the evening of Saturday 13th April 1963 is one of them in the shape of O4 No.63701 (there was another O4 in front, sadly unidentified), a visitor from Staveley which had spent the whole of its main line railway life on the ER and the LNER Southern Area. One of the bargain buys from the Ministry of Munitions in the 1920s, this 2-8-0 had been built in July 1918 by Robert Stephenson & Co. and became MofM No.1684. When the LNER acquired it and refurbished it in 1925, it was renumbered 6498. In May 1946 it became 3701, and then 63701 in September 1950. The O4 had spent twenty-two years working from sheds on the former Great Eastern section of the Southern Area of the LNER before transferring to Mexborough and 'friendly faces' in October 1951. It went to Staveley in February 1962 as operations at Mexborough wound down but when Staveley also became a victim of the closures and so-called 'rationalisation' it found a new home at Langwith Junction in June 1965, only to be condemned when it got there! Handsome engines from any angle, the LNER and BR certainly got their worth out of them. Most of the locomotives within this scene are goods engines which helped to give York a sense of variety amongst the numerous visitors and residents at 50A. *N.W.Skinner (ARPT)*.

One year and one week later, many of York's resident engines have been laid up or simply condemned. The date is 18th April 1964, another Saturday, and its evening too. This melancholy line consists four V2s, a B16, and a WD 2-8-0; alongside but hidden behind is a similar line-up. No.60925 is the only one identified but it was a York engine for the whole of its twenty-three years life. On this day it was still in Capital stock and it would be another five weeks before it was condemned. In August it was taken to Swindon for disposal. Having visited York North depot on the same day as the photographer, I can confirm that the following V2s were also 'stored' on the two tracks in question: Nos.60833, 60855, 60856, 60932, and 60975. Although there was a reasonable number of the class still active at this time, the mighty V2s had had their day and various scrapyards beckoned throughout the land. *C.J.B.Sanderson (ARPT)*.

North shed yard in the early 1950s with an interesting bunch of locomotives gathered around a water column. On the left is a WD 2-8-0, Garratt No.47984 (the only one identifiable), and a B16. On the right we have another WD 2-8-0 and a B16. Remember walking down these rows of engines looking up and never, it seems, looking at the ground and where we were placing our feet? Did anyone ever fall? It seems not. Now this is one scene which could not be re-enacted today, for at least three reasons. *K.H.Cockerill (ARPT)*.

York was never blessed with any Gresley Pacifics of its own during BR days, indeed when Nationalisation dawned, York had just two Pacifics allocated – a pair of Thompson A2/3s. However Gresley Pacifics certainly visited the depot and in August 1952 Carlisle Canal's No.60068 SIR VISTO is seen being readied by its driver whilst the A3 was en route to Carlisle after a General overhaul at Doncaster. This engine was one of the original A1s and was rebuilt during 1948 to A3 standard. It had spent the whole of its life in what was essentially the Scottish Area of the LNER and later the Scottish Region of BR (shed boundary changes in the 1950s effectively brought Canal shed, and Kingmoor, into the London Midland Region but for all intents and purposes all of Canal's workings took engines north of Carlisle, into Scottish Region), Canal shed being its home from November 1940 until condemned on 1st October 1962. So, this particular A3 was something of a rarity, in this part of the world, and only put in an appearance during works visits. Note the lack of paint on the front numberplate – quite an oversight by the painters at Doncaster perhaps? *K.H.Cockerill (ARPT)*.

59

Showing the results of a slight front end impact (nowt to do with us at 50A!), V2 No.60800 GREEN ARROW is driven slowly up the shed yard circa 1952 (the modified pony truck was fitted as per Casual Light repair of February 1952). The engine is turned, coaled (quantity not quality appears to be the maxim), watered and ready to work back home to London where explanations about that bent bit would be required. *E.H.Cockerill (ARPT)*.

Although some Thompson L1s were allocated to NE Region depots – and just about everywhere else east of Birmingham – York never possessed any. However, because of its strategic position on the main line, York often hosted visitors, which were either en route to Darlington for overhaul or returning to their home sheds after works attention. Such appears to be the case here in the 1950s when No.67774 was stabled over the ash pits at York whilst apparently on its way to Darlington. It was usual to let these engines work their passage from Southern Area sheds, or at least make their own way rather than be towed. Whatever the date, this 2-6-4T was working from London sheds for the whole of its life except for the last eight months which were spent at Grantham. The shedplate seems to read 34E which would put it at Neasden (21/12/49-1/7/51 & 11/11/51-30/9/56), but it may well be 34B Hornsey (1/7/51-11/11/51), or it might possibly be 34A (30/9/56-21/5/61)? Sorry for the uncertainty but it all adds to the magic of the hobby. *C.J.B.Sanderson (ARPT)*.

York's long tradition as a centre for carriage and wagon building, and repairing, must not be forgotten during our brief stop-over in the city. (*above*) Hardly looking smart and certainly past its best, this former North Eastern passenger vehicle was seconded into Internal Use only at some stage of its career and on 9th September 1960 it was in use as a canteen vehicle at York North/Clifton/Leeman Road motive power depot, stabled alongside the aforementioned thoroughfare. Just when the ex-carriage was employed and for how long in such salubrious surroundings is uncertain but it may well have got the job when work started rebuilding the engine sheds in 1957; its redundancy no doubt commenced when the building work was completed. Note the water tower which was a guiding beacon for enthusiasts on their first-time visit to the shed. (*opposite, top*) This former NER Parcels van was condemned on 28th July 1962 according to the legend. The picture was taken the day afterwards but the vehicle should have been condemned years ago judging by its appearance. Although there are various legends on its flanks: 'Painters' and 'Return to Leeman Rd Storeyard York' there is no identification. Nevertheless, a handsome vehicle – once! (*opposite*) Another passenger bogie which had also been a Brake in its heyday. Ex-NER, it is identified as DE900129 and has the same 'Return...' legend along with 'D.E.Painters York'. What did the painters get in exchange I wonder? All of these pieces of rolling stock probably started life at York Carriage works and it seems they were to end it there too. *all N.W.Skinner (ARPT)*.

62

Heaton V2 No.60810 is making light work of this northbound parcels train as it rushes through Benningborough circa 1949. The original station at this location was opened in March 1841 but much of what we see here was the result of the 1900s widening by the North Eastern Railway. Like many railway stations on BR, Benningborough was not named after the nearest settlement, Benningborough village was in fact nearly two miles away, by road, to the south west, about one mile as the crow flies! The population of the village at the time of the NER widening was a mere 55 souls, whereas half a mile immediately east of the station was another village called Shipton which could boast more than 300 inhabitants, a main road – A19 – post office, church, pubs, etc. The clue to the naming of the railway station perhaps lay in the fact that a certain Benningborough Hall, beside the River Ouse to the west, was not too far away. Even nearer was Benningborough Grange but for now that is enough factual about the lye of the land and the local 'owners' because it is beginning to make this caption sound a bit 'foreign' methinks. The station closed from 15th September 1958. *J.W.Armstrong (ARPT)*.

Tollerton was another of the stations brought into use when the main line was opened in 1841 and, like Benningborough, it too was altered substantially at the turn of the century by the NER as a result of the quadrupling of the main line north of York to a point just south of Alne. The bridge in the background, which linked the nearby (four hundred yards away) village of Tollerton (pop.500+) with the A19 trunk road, was the demarcation line of the 1st and 2nd stations here, the original station being largely located south of the bridge. The Down platform surface appears to be composed of nothing more than trodden earth which may well have been the case. Passenger numbers here, probably at any time in the life of the station, would hardly have been a threat to the integrity of the platform surface anyway, paved or not. Running with a good head of steam, Thompson B1 No.61274 has charge of a northbound freight in this undated photograph which was recorded on a winter's afternoon before September 1958. Note the signal box at the south end of the Down platform; this box apparently played no part in the main line signalling and was used only for local goods movements. Bucking the trend of 1958 closures (it was not required to change the already quadruple layout), Tollerton station remained open for business until 1st November 1965, when it became a deserved victim of Doctor Beeching? How it remained open for so many years is baffling because from June 1952 it was served by just two Up trains on weekdays (three on Saturdays), and three Down trains (four on Saturdays). Things only got worse in February 1953 when the Pickering passenger service was abandoned and Tollerton was served by a single Up and Down service each morning except Sundays (there had been no Sunday service since 1943). In August 1959 further madness set in when the Up passenger service was discontinued; the northbound stopper remained faithful as it was apparently delivering parcels. A survey carried out in the week ending 11th July 1964 found that one passenger boarded a train here whilst one alighted. The week ending 24th October 1964 found that not one person had used the station! *J.F.Sedgwick (ARPT)*.

65

Darlington based B1 No.61020 GEMSBOK runs through Raskelf with an Up passenger train circa 1956. This engine was no stranger to this stretch of the ECML having been built at Darlington and then served the following sheds up to June 1958: Heaton, Darlington, York, Neville Hill, York, and Darlington, in that order. After a spell at Low Moor and Wakefield, it returned to York in September 1960 and finally ended its days being cut up in January 1963 where it had all started – Darlington. Raskelf station had a much longer career and was amongst the passenger venues for the opening of the line in 1841. It remained untouched until the 1930s LNER widening of this section of the ECML; the changes are evident with the concrete platform sections on the left and the staggered platform layout (the additional Down line was beyond the platform on the left). Once again, Monday 5th May 1958 figures large for that station because like many others of its ilk on this part of the line, it too was closed (Saturday 3rd May was the last time that any trains called here and the station was locked up after the last train departed on that final Saturday). This station was another of those built virtually in the middle of nowhere; the settlement after which it was named was over a mile away (pop.450+), and nearer to the A19 trunk road. Admitted, when the builders of that dead-straight and virtually level racing track planned their route all those decades ago, they were obviously thinking of the through traffic linking the cities and large towns rather than the meagre traffic to be had from the occasional rural passenger. Of course part of the deal with the landowners was to provide a station for their convenience too; it took nearly 120 years before common sense was finally allowed to blossom. We have now reached the 201 mile mark since leaving King's Cross and it was round about here where engine crews used to change over on the non-stops. *J.W.Armstrong (ARPT)*.

66

Here is the first real illustration to portrait the presence of the racetrack section north of York. A4 No.60032 GANNET has charge of the Down working of *THE NORTHUMBRIAN* and is producing a nice exhaust which gives the impression of speed. We are at Pilmoor station during a late afternoon in the autumn of 1949 with low sun and a slight easterly breeze. Now this station was remote, even compared with the others so far reviewed, in that it had no road connections, the only way to and from the place was by train. Up until 1953 Pilmoor was the ECML railhead for the branch line from Boroughbridge, that connection having been established in 1847 when the station came into operation. The branch line slewed south-west from a platform out of sight on the cameraman's right. Trains from Thirsk to Pickering and vice versa also called, which perhaps lessened the isolation of the platforms somewhat. During 1933 the ECML was widened here by the addition of a new Down line, nearest the camera, but widening was to take place again when BR closed the station in May 1958, along with the others to the south which closed at the same time, to carry out the works which included adding a new Up slow line as far as Alne and therefore completing the four-track section from Northallerton to York. North of Pilmoor the line had been quadrupled as far as Thirsk in 1942 by the addition of new Up and Down slow lines. Note that the station still has oil lamp illumination, a feature of all the stations south of here as far as York. The Grantham Pacific looks the business especially in the dark blue livery with black and white lining, a colour scheme applied whilst the A4 was in works 3rd May to 10th June 1949. It seems incredible to realise that No.60032 was only eleven years old when this scene was recorded. The naming of the train depicted was a BR innovation of an existing service; it was named in time for the first winter service workings on 26th September 1949 (10 a.m. Newcastle–King's Cross and the 12.20 p.m. King's Cross–Newcastle). *J.W.Hague.*

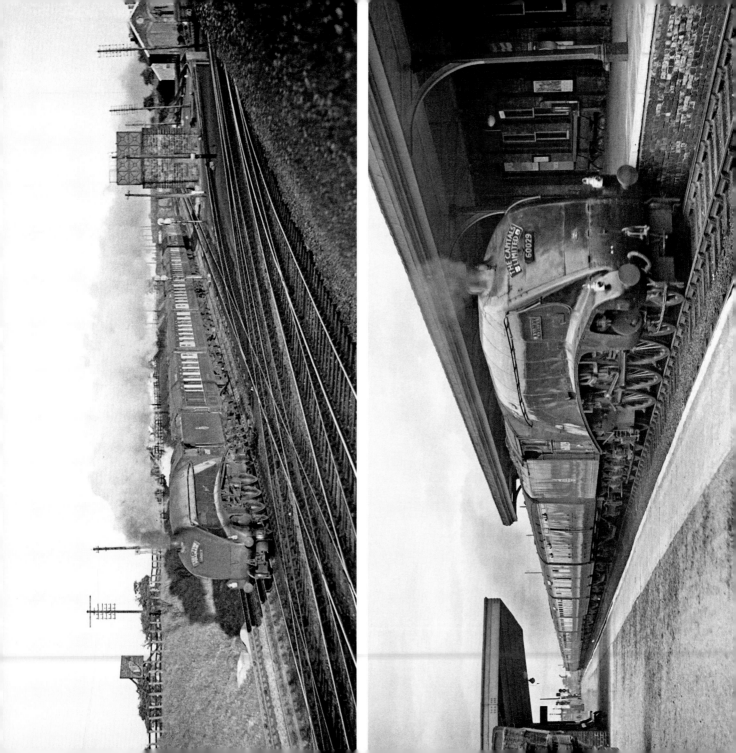

(*opposite, top*) Thirsk – early 1950s – with A4 No.60017 SILVER FOX running through the junction in fine style whilst heading the Down *TEES-TYNE PULLMAN*. The Pacific still has the long guard irons (removed June 1953) and also has the experimental ATC (fitted September 1950) and, it appears to be wearing the Dark blue livery with black and white lining (applied at same time as ATC fitted). So, although we can date the picture within that two and a half years time frame, we can't be any more precise than that. However, it is a glorious picture from that golden age. *J.W.Hague (ARPT)*. (*opposite, bottom*) Before it became *THE ELIZABETHAN*, the Edinburgh-London non-stop in British Railways days was titled *THE CAPITALS LIMITED* and here at Thirsk – circa 1952 – the Up train is hammering through the station with 'Top Shed' A4 No.60029 WOODCOCK in charge of the twelve coach formation. Both platforms became islands when the quadrupling took place, the original faces serving the fast lines and the new, outer faces, the slow lines. Today only the outer faces remain, the platforms originally serving the fast lines being cut back considerably, and fenced off for safety purposes. *J.W.Hague (ARPT)*. (*above*) B16 No.61424 heads a northbound freight on the Down slow and through the junction with the Melmerby line at Thirsk circa 1952 which would place the 4-6-0 on Neville Hill's allocation. The line from Thirsk to Melmerby (coming in from the right) closed to both passenger and goods traffic from 14th September 1959 and was lifted shortly afterwards west of the junction from Thirsk (Town) goods; the spur from the ECML to that goods junction was left in situ until the end of 1966. This arguably left BR bereft of another suitable diversion route for the Leeds–Ripon–Northallerton traffic in the event of accident or maintenance purposes but that was only the start of things to come. In the distance can be seen a bridge spanning the ECML and just beyond that another bridge. This latter bridge carried the 1848 line of the Leeds & Thirsk Railway into a terminus which became known as Thirsk (Town) – the main line station was known as Thirsk (Junction) but that was never timetabled as such – but it was a short lived passenger station closing in December 1855. The goods facility remained in use until 3rd October 1966, some 111 years later. *J.W.Hague*.

We have no details for the three illustrations presented on these two pages, except for the location, and the date is set somewhere in the mid 1950s. We are at Otterington, some 214 miles from King's Cross, looking north towards Northallerton. Otterington station is immediately behind the cameraman and was probably still open for business when these images were recorded. The nearest settlement is South Otterington with a population of approximately 300, located half a mile west of the station but not wholly reliant on the train services because the A167 road passes through the village and offered a decent bus service for the locals. The station opened with the line in 1841 and was altered considerably when the main line was quadrupled in 1933. Closer came on 15th September 1958; its meagre clientele no longer being a strain on NE Region finances. Working in a clockwise direction (sorry but all three trains are heading south) we have Peppercorn A1 No.60147 NORTH EASTERN (*above*) heading a King's Cross bound express with apparent little effort being shown. The Pacific looks rather smart and considering that it was a Gateshead engine at this time, it was probably ex-works; although I stand to be corrected for my bout of cynicism. (*opposite, top*) Also using the Up fast, this unidentified van train was probably the Newcastle–Manchester (Red Bank Siding) newspaper empties, its rich mix of vehicles being enough to keep any carriage fan happy. At York the NE power, consisting B1 No.61071 and A2/2 No.60501 COCK O' THE NORTH would be exchanged for LM Region engines; the contrasting external condition of the two Pacifics is noticeable, the latter being a York engine at the time, as was the B1! (*opposite*) This train of iron ore empties had just joined the main line at Northallerton after its run from Tees-side. B16 No.61465 is finding it easy going with this lot but the Down loaded trains required a bit more power if progress was to be maintained in a reasonable time. A LM Garratt would probably be waiting for this train on its arrival in York. Oh yes, the B16 was also from 50A. *all J.W.Hague.*

The sign says it all, as does that 1933 signal box! So, we have reached the end of another stage in our epic journey along the ECML and all these people have come out to greet us. The event, if there was one, is unrecorded, as is the date, but the motive power was J21 No.65038 a Northallerton engine from May 1952 to withdrawal in November 1954. A couple of schoolboys join some older enthusiasts but the overwhelming impression is the number of railwaymen on the platform; not just station staff but footplatemen, fitters and probably shunters – I wonder why? The cameraman was Ken Cockerill who was known for being jovial and funny at times and, judging by the smiling faces of the railwaymen, he had just cracked a funny. Note that not a single cigarette is to be seen – most unusual for the period which was circa 1952? *K.H.Cockerill (ARPT).*